Dining With Dub

W.A. FRANKLIN "DUB"

iUniverse, Inc.
New York   Bloomington

Dining With Dub

The views expressed in this work are solely those of the author
and do not necessarily reflect the views of the publisher, and the
publisher hereby disclaims any responsibility for them.

iUniverse books may be ordered through booksellers or by contacting:

iUniverse
1663 Liberty Drive
Bloomington, IN 47403
www.iuniverse.com
1-800-Authors (1-800-288-4677)

Because of the dynamic nature of the Internet, any Web addresses or
links contained in this book may have changed since publication and
may no longer be valid. The views expressed in this work are solely those
of the author and do not necessarily reflect the views of the publisher,
and the publisher hereby disclaims any responsibility for them.

ISBN: 978-1-4401-2220-0 (pbk)
ISBN: 978-1-4401-2221-7 (ebk)

Printed in the United States of America

iUniverse rev. date: 7/15/2009

Contents

THIS RECIPE WAS ONE THAT I MADE UP FROM AN ODD RECIPE ON A CAN WITH A SUGGESTION AND A LITTLE IMAGINATION, A BIG FAMILY DINNER WAS BEING PLANNED AT OUR HOUSE AND THE ENTRÉE WAS A SLOW COOKED BEEF ROAST. IT WAS ALL JUST IN THE PLANNING STAGE AND THERE WERE LOTS OF IDEAS FLOATING AROUND. ONE THAT CAUGHT MY EYE WAS SOME GOOD BAKED BEANS. I SAID NOTHING BUT THE IDEAS WERE GOING ON IN MY HEAD.

I WAS IN THE GROCERY STORE AND WHEN I CAME TO THE CANNED BEANS I STOPPED AND READ THEM ALL. WHEN I GOT HOME I HAD TWO CANS OF CAMPBELL'S PORK AND BEANS. I ALSO HAD A RECIPE OF SORTS.

USING A 2 QUART BAKING DISH I POURED ONE OF THE CANS IN AFTER REMOVING THE LITTLE PIECES OF FAT. OVER THIS LAYER OF BEANS I PUT IN THE ONION, CATSUP, DRY MUSTARD AND BROWN SUGAR. I PUT THE OTHER CAN OF BEANS IN AND ON TOP OF THIS I PLACED TWO STRIPS BACON.

I BAKED IT UNCOVERED IN A PRE HEATED OVEN AT 325 DEGREES FOR 45 MINUTES.

THESE INGREDIENTS AND MEASUREMENTS ARE NOT ABSOLUTE. YOU CAN CHANGE THEM TO SUIT YOUR TASTE.

2 15 0/Z CAN CAMPBELL PORK AND BEANS

1 TBS DRIED ONION

2 TBS CATSUP

½ TSP DRY MUSTARD

2 STRIPS BACON. .

BREAKFAST BURRITO

2 large eggs ready to scramble

½ cup breakfast meat chopped

Some dried onion for flavor

2 large flour tortillas

Hash brown potatoes

Fry the hash browns and meat individually. Put the chopped meat and onion in with the eggs. Put the hash browns on first then the eggs. Use salsa or hot sauce if desired. Salt and pepper?

Here is the true story as testimony as to how good these can really be. Last summer I needed two on my grandsons to do some yard work for me. Only one was available but his best bud would come along. He is a guy that lives on potato chips and Coke. I lined them up on what I needed done and went to fix them some breakfast. Brett said it would be a waste of time fixing his friend any. I fixed four and served them with a glass of cold milk.

What I heard was that Bretts friend went home and told his mother all about what he had eaten and asked her to fix that kind of food for him.

BUTTER MILK CHICKEN

This is a simple," why didn't I think of it recipe?" The breast is usually the most popular part of the chicken so I watch and when the grocery store that I shop at has them on sale, I buy. They have the bone in but with a sharp boning knife they are easily deboned. They are pretty thick so I split them and make twice as many servings.

Take a bowl and pour in some butter milk. Put your chicken in and coat it well and then coat the wet chicken with the cracker or bread crumbs that we made earlier. It will not work on any other type meat. Fry it in a hot skillet. It doesn't take long to cook chicken..

Do you want to know how to keep that head of lettuce you just bought fresher longer. Put it in a brown paper bag. I don't know why it works, it just does.

SWEET AND SOUR PORK

In the old house we lived in for 20 years we had a tradition. All of my family gathered on Easter Sunday and we cooked and ate Chinese food. Most of the adults did the cooking. Paul made Chop Suey, Cathy the egg rolls and so on. Me, I did the sweet and sour pork. Of course I never made enough for any one to get a second shot. I made a crock pot full of the stuff. This is a recipe for four people. You can see how easy it is to increase.

1 pound pork shoulder

Corn starch

1 cup pineapple [cubed]

1 green pepper diced

½ cup cider vinegar

¼ cup firmly packed brown sugar

¾ cup water

1 tbs molasses

Slice the meat about ¼ inch thick. Dredge in corn starch. Fry on both sides in hot grease. While this is happening mix all of the other ingredients When you have removed all the grease you can from the meat with a paper towel, put it in the pot. Keep hot but do not bring to a boil.

If you have a double boiler this is a good time to use it. You won't be constantly nagged about stirring.

Put one table spoon butter in the pot and stir in one table spoon sf flour. When mixed well stir in enough milk to make white sauce and then add a cup of that cheese that you have stored. You can add milk or cheese and make it as thick or thin as you want.

Peeling garlic can be a real chore if you just try and peel it. That is the way I used to do it. If I had a lot to peel, it took for ever. Not any more. There are at least two ways to simplify this task.

One way is to lay the clove of garlic down and press down with the heel of your hand until you hear a crackling sound. The other way is to hold the clove with both hands and gently twist until you hear that sound. Either way the skins will just slip right off and life gets a lot simpler.

Want to make the vegetables in your veggie bin last longer? Line the bin with paper towels.

A STAR IS BORN

Easter Sunday and our forty forth wedding anniversary were on the same day and the kids had a big week end planned. On Saturday they had as much of the whole family together as they could. Before dinner we were going to have a big baseball game. I was going to umpire. The rules for the little ones was to keep swinging until they hit the ball then run like your cat runs when a dog is chasing it. An inning would last until all the team had a turn at bat or there were three outs.

Me, I was ready. "PLAY BALL".

The game was see-sawing back and forth with half the players not even listening to my calls. Then it became Ryan's turn at bat. He is seven years old and the youngest player. Ryan took a couple of practice swings and stepped up to the plate. One of our other daughters had asked Ryan's mother why she had not introduced him to T-Ball? She answered that she could not afford it....

We were at strike four or five when we all heard it. Not a loud crack, but it was a hit. Ryan dropped his bat and was on his way. The catcher, pitcher and third base man were all waiting on the other to pick up the ball. Finally the third base man grabbed it and in his haste missed first base all together. Ryan was just steps away and half of the in field was all scrambling for the ball.

When Ryan's foot hit the base and there was no one there he just made a left turn and headed for second. Now here is a kid who has a love affair with dirt and is always in trouble for playing in it at the wrong time. Second base was wide open and chances were he could of made it to third, but seeing all that dirt was just too much of a temptation so Ryan slid in to second feet first just like the pros do it. He immediately stood and dusted him self off. He had taken on at least a pound of that wonderful dirt but only found it necessary to dust out a couple of ounces...................

Neither the short stop or second base man had seen him arrive after being involved in the bad throw so they just ignored him. Ryan, forgetting that while on base one of your jobs was to worry the heck out of the pitcher by acting like you were going to run just stood there like a statue, but he was ready.

Finally some one got a base hit and Ryan was off like a rocket. Seeing all that good dirt at third base and not even knowing where the ball was or who had it and being invisible (or so it seemed), he just naturally slid into third base taking on another pound of dirt. Going through the same ritual as before, he beat out another two ounces of dirt. At this rate there won't be enough dirt left in Visalia to grow weeds. The next batter up was a heavy hitter. He is on the varsity team at Redwood High School. On the second pitch he connected and as before Ryan didn't even look. He just took off and was sliding across home plate, taking on another pound of dirt before the ball ever hit the ground.

I guess he was getting heavy with all that extra weight he had picked up going around the bases because this time he slapped a half pound or so out of his clothes. I guess its not as much fun getting dirty when it is O.K.

Ryan was walking back to the dug-out and I was so proud of him that ---

---WHOOPS------- was that a swagger I saw in his walk? Well why not. Ryan had just taken one of those mini steps a boy has to take while reaching for manhood that all too often go unnoticed...........................

CHILI BEANS

1 pound any red bean

6 cup water

1 pound extra lean hamburger

2 large cloves garlic minced

1 small yellow onion chopped

1 15 o/z can diced tomatoes

1/3 cup chili powder

2 tsp paprika

2 tsp cumin

Wash the beans and soak them in several cups of water over night. This makes them cook faster.

I ate other peoples beans for years and sometimes I asked what was in them and some times I figured it out for myself. Most of them were pretty much alike and left something yet to be discovered.

My beans had soaked all night and the water was all gone so I added the rest and started them cooking. When they were closer to being done I added the onion, garlic and tomatoes. I then crumbled the hamburger as small as I could right into to the beans. Forget the frying and sautéing. That was where extra grease was added. I then put the rest of the ingredients in and turned the fire down to low and simmered this for an hour or so. The first time I purposely put the lid on the pot and left the beans sitting there over night. The next morning I looked and there was very little suet on top of my beans.

CHILIMALE

One day I had made a pot of chili beans. We needed to go to the store and on the way home I stopped at a take out Mexican store and purchased a dozen tamales. When we were home I was preparing our supper by putting chili beans on a tamale and my sister and brother-in law stopped at our house. I insisted that they sit and eat. Helen, Darlene and I had eaten two each and we were watching Paul eat his third one when he looked up and started to apologize. Having been raised on a lot of beans he changed his mind and asked what I called this. " Chilimales was my answer "..........!

TAMALE PIE

When Helen and I got married I told her she could cook any thing she wanted as long as it was not tamale pie. Her answer was that if she makes it I will eat it and I did. This is actually my mothers recipe.

1 lb ground meat

3 tsp chopped yellow onion

2 tsp oil

2 ½ cups canned tomatoes chopped

½ cup corn meal

¾ cup whole kernel canned corn

2 large eggs beaten

2tsp salt [?]

1 tsp each paprika and chili powder

Pepper to taste

Fry meat and onion in oil and drain excess grease. Add tomatoes. Bring to a boil. Add corn meal 1 tsp at a time siring constantly for 10 minutes.

Add remaining ingredients and blend thoroughly. Pour mixture into a greased pan and bake an hour at 325 degrees

This recipe was handed down to me from my Father who had received it from his good friend Gus. WW2 was finally over and the Great Depression was fast becoming a bad memory. Life was getting good and people were walking around with some money in their pockets and a lot of new businesses were springing up all over the place. Gus was one of those who wanted to start his own Chili stand, but Gus did not want the responsibility of a whole building. In the pool hall there was a counter about 10 feet long that was not in use. After discussing it with the owner Gus set himself up in business and started cooking his Chili. The place stopped smelling like a pool hall and started smelling like a restaurant.

All of a sudden you could stop playing pool and eat a bowl of really good chili. Next door was a bar and they also had a counter with a fellow who made the best Lima Beans and Ham Hocks. There were several orange packing houses in the area so during the season if you wanted a bowl of either you had better have it before noon because exactly at noon the workers boiled out of those packing houses and by one-o-clock there was nothing left.

What I changed in this recipe was to remove a lot of the suet that Dad and Gus thought was needed. Actually that is where you get some of the flavor from but, you do not need it to have a bowl of good Chili. If you do not know what suet is. It is the hard fat found around organs. It is what our Great Grand Mothers used to make candles. 3 ½ ounces of raw suet has 854 calories.......

10 pounds chili meat

5-6 cloves garlic minced

2 base ball sized yellow onion chopped

1 tsp salt

4 cups water

In a large pot mix these ingredients together with your clean hand. Cook slowly using a low flame. Stir and breakup often so it will cook evenly. When done add the following and again cook slowly until it cooks down a ½ inch or so. ¾ cup chili powder, 1/3 cup paprika and 1/3 cup cumin.

CORN BEEF HASH

Walking my mail route one day I got to thinking about corn beef hash so on the way home, I stopped at the store and bought some. The next morning I was eating some with a pair of over easy eggs when true to my luck I bit into a foreign object that turned out to be a piece of metal

I am the guy that always is the lucky recipient. My wife thinks it is funny. Well I quit eating and went to work about half mad and half hungry. I made up my mind that day to learn how the stuff is made.

I made some mistakes like cutting the meat too small, using too much cream and finding the right potato was a struggle. Here is what I came up with and it is pretty good.

Pick out a brisket that serves your purpose. Make corn beef and cabbage and what is left goes for the hash. Put the brisket fat side down in a pot and make sure it is covered with water. Cook it until it is done. I use my grease separator on the liquid before I put my cabbage in to cook.

In a large bowl dice 2 15 o/z cans of potatoes. That is right, I found that the canned ones are a lot firmer and easier to cut up. Add a small chopped onion and your diced meat. Get it all coated with cream. Put some butter in a nine inch skillet and pour in your mixture. Pack it down real good and turn the fire down kind of low. When the smell of cooking onions is strong it is time to turn it over. When you can't smell onions cooking any more it is usually because it is done. It should be nice and brown............................

Did you ever wonder why they call it the World Series? When and where did they play base ball with any other Worldly countries?

Why do you think Mars Candy calls one of its candy bars the Three Musketeers? Could it be that at the beginning you actually had three small bars? Hummmmm

Now why the heck does this recipe call for some sort of crumbs when I don't even have any? How many times have you felt like that? Here is my solution. For cracker crumbs take a tube of crackers and place them in a large zip lock bag. Get out your rolling pin and start rolling. You can make your crumbs as course or fine as you want. Seasoning can be added.

Bread crumbs are a little harder. Take a few slices of old bread and place it on your cookie sheet. Turn your oven on to warm and place the cookie sheet in the oven. Cook for about 30 minutes and then turn off the oven. Leave the bread in the oven for a day or so and you will have what they call hard tack. Do it the same way you did the crackers.

BISCUIT'S

Our Grand Mothers of old invented Bisquick by cutting there lard into there flour to keep out the weavels. All she had to do was add baking soda and some liquid and biscuits were just minutes away.

My brother in law told me his secrete. Add a little extra liquid, I use butter milk before you knead in the flour. You have to handle it carefully though. As moist as the dough is you could make it into dumplings. They sure turn out good.

Some Of Life's Lessons

1937
Second grade

Noon recess and you have just been dared to moon some girls. What seven year old can resist a dare like that? We don't even like girls so down came the pants followed by the screams. You would have thought they were being shot at or worse. Recess ended and classes resumed. The event that took place in the school yard was forgotten until the door opened and Mrs Glenn the principle was filling it and asking me of all people to come with her. Lesson number one was about to be fulfilled.

Mrs Glenn ask me if I had in fact lowered my pants in front of some girls? I could see that lying was not going to get me any thing but more trouble, so I answered yes. With that part over Mrs Glenn asked me to lower them again. I was being spanked and she was trying to be gentle so I gave it every thing I had to give. Lesson number one was think before you accept a dare. Lesson two was a short time away.

After having experienced total embarrassment at school I had decided to not say any thing about it when I got home. What the heck, it was over and would soon be forgotten so just leave it alone. Ha! I had a big surprise waiting for me just inside the front door. Total Doom and Destruction that looked exactly like my mother was what was waiting and I just walked right into all of it.

"You have embarrassed the whole family. You know better than to pull a stunt like that. When I am through with you you'll think twice before doing it again,"

Well, I only thought Mrs Glenn spanked me. Mother was going for an Olympian Gold Medal and I'm sure she won it hands down. I guess Double Jeopardy wasn't around yet.

Many, many years later I was talking to Mother and she brought it up and said that Mrs Glenn said I acted like she was beating me to death.

I was raised up eating egg plant that was sliced, dredged in flour and fried in hot grease. As far as I knew that was the standard way to fix egg plant. Sometimes the slices were so big you could only cook one at a time. When you were finally done the first ones cooked were getting cold. There had to be a better way.

One day I treated an egg plant like I was making mashed potatoes only when I mashed them I added a slightly beaten egg and some corn meal. I let it set for a while until the corn meal swelled some and I could mold it into patties. I then placed these patties in a skillet with hot grease and browned them swiftly. When we ate them that old greasy taste was no longer in them.

It is hard to say how much corn meal to use. It would depend on how big your egg plant is.............................

Try adding some sautéed onion and bacon some time...........!

EGGS BOARDING HOUSE

Nothing about this tasty breakfast is mine. My wife and I spent the weekend with some friends about 25 years ago and this is what was served Sunday morning. The lady of the house used her biscuit cutter and cut a hole in a slice of bread. She buttered both sides of the bread and placed it in a hot skillet. She then dropped an egg in that hole and when it was done on one side she flipped it over and cooked the other side. Boy was it good.

HOT DOG AND HAMBURGER RELISH

Ever notice how the wiener takes up most of the space allowed in the bun and you have to balance the add on's? Not any more for me. I don't buy those jars that take up space while you are not using them. Make your own.

For the hot dog chop some onion and add it to some mustard, mayo and sweet relish.

For the hamburger chop some onion and add it to some catsup. Mayo and dill relish

How much of every thing to add depends up on how many you are fixing.

The good thing about doing your own canning is that you can pronounce all the ingredients and they are for every day use.

GOULASH

This is another one of those easy dishes.

½ pound lean hamburger

½ pint salsa

1 8 o/z can tomato sauce

1 can water

3 o/z any kind of macaroni

Growing up during and after the Great Depression Mothers had two ways of using hamburger. Meat loaf and hamburgers. You can see that my experience with hamburger started out to be limited but I was going to learn some new ways. Having a wife and three children is a lot of mouth's to feed, money was always scarce and hamburger was cheap.

By now I had eaten hamburger a number of ways and knew that help was on the way. One day I crumbled my meat in the skillet cooked it and rid myself of the excess grease. I poured in all the above ingredients and while this was slowly cooking I cooked the macaroni. Cooking macaroni is easy. Boil 2 cups of water, add the macaroni and put the lid on the pot. Set it a side for 30 minutes and it is done. Pour the water off the macaroni and replace it with the skillet contents, stir it well........

THE NEW SHIRT'S

At the Post Office every one starts as the bottom substitute and we all get the same amount of money for our clothing allotment which means that for the first two years you have to really watch when you order so you get the clothes and shoes you need. The first year is really the worst. Two pair of pants and three shirts was all I could scrape by on. My wife Helen tried ever so hard to make me out to be the poster boy for the Post Office so She just washed those pour shirts to death. The collars busted and were turned and they were bursting again when my boss Mark called me to one side and asked me a question. He asked me to not get upset by it and I said I would not. "Is that the best shirt you have?"

No, I have two more at home just like it was my answer. Mark said that if I would sign a purchase order he and the Post Master would see that I received three new shirts. I did not mention this to Helen and time passed. One day a parcel was left at my station and I knew it contained the new shirts. I took it home and when I entered the house I handed it to Helen. Of course she asked what was in it so I told her to open it and see.

"Oh Boy, new shirts." I need to wash these. Dub can't stand sizing or starch she was saying as she left the room and me just standing there.

GREEN BEANS ALA DUB

When I was growing up I hated green beans . It was an awful smell when they were cooking. Women thought you had to cook them a lot longer than was necessary. We were in the grips of the Great Depression and food was some times hard to come by so you just kept your mouth shut and eat. I thought the only way I would ever get away from that smell was to grow up and leave home. Ha.

I did grow up and Uncle Sam needed me and guess what? The mess sergeant just loved to feed us green beans only they were canned and did not smell as bad.

It wasn't until I was married and had children that I got serious about fixing them a better way. The darn things are too good to be ignored.

One day in the kitchen I chopped two slices of bacon, diced some onion and garlic. I fried the bacon almost done, added the onion and garlic and let them sauté I then stirred in a 15o/z can of green beans. I turned the fire down low and set them cook slowly. I added some water several times and when I was satisfied they were ready they were a little wrinkled and boy o boy were they ever good...............

Of all my recipes this one is the absolute favorite. This is how it began. Once upon a time I had a big garden spot for my wife Helen to have her kitchen garden. I kept it weeded and watered. One year I planted 3 kinds of squash. One evening we sat down to supper and with out thinking Helen had prepared 3 kinds of squash 3 different ways. We all five laughed and ate a healthy meal. [Wish I had thought up that once upon a time thing]

2 slices bacon chopped

¼ cup onion diced

Some garlic diced

3 kinds med sized squash cut up

1 14 ½ can stewed tomatoes

1 can water

Fry the bacon and saute the onion and garlic. While this is going on take a 2 quart bowl and empty the can of tomatoes and the water in it. Cut up the squash and add them to the bowl. Mix the bowl contents evenly and add to hot 9 inch skillet. Turn the fire down and cook slowly. ....

HASH BROWNS

There are not too many ways to prepare hash browns but here is my favorite. I guess I am a little odd because I like to use canned potatoes. Ill bet a lot of you did not know they even exist. They seem to me to be a lot firmer and shred better. I just shred as much as I need on some wax paper, sprinkle in a little dried onion and a little flour making sure to mix it a little. Melt a pat of butter in your egg skillet and pour the potatoes in. Keep the fire low and fix the rest of your meal. You have just browned the potatoes on one side so just plop them out brown side up and divide them.................

FRIED POTATOES

When you fry potatoes do you have trouble turning them over and end up getting them all the same golden brown. Well I did too until I watched closely while my Father fried some potatoes. After he had them all cut up and ready for the skillet he sprinkled some flour over them, stirred them some and put them in. When they were brown on one side he turned the whole thing over and browned the other side. Out of the skillet they were beautiful. When asked he told me that the flour works as a catalyst and holds the potatoes together. Amazing......................................

HUSH PUPPIES

2 cups corn meal
¼ cup flour
1 tsp baking soda
1 tsp baking powder
1 tsp salt
½ cup diced onion
1 ¼ cup butter milk
1 large egg

Mix all the dry ingredients together. In a bowl mix the egg and butter milk. Stir in the dry ingredients and mix well. Make into teaspoon size balls and drop into hot grease. Cook until golden brown.

Texas Style

Add 1 cup canned whole corn
3 strips fried bacon crumbled
1 tablespoon minced hot pepper

WHOOP'S

It was during one of the two delicious times of the year. You know, during spring and fall when you feel like you are getting even with the utility companies by neither heating or cooling. This happened to be in October.

In the business part of my mail route are a group of office buildings, most of them belong to dentists. When the weather is this nice you do not think of closing the door when you enter because you are going to go right back out that same door.

The door to this dentist office opened off the right to the west wall. Where the door stops there is a rack attached to the wall holding information packets. While entering a lady sitting against the east wall stood up and walked in front of me going to that rack. Knowing where she was I completely dismissed her from my mind. I placed the daily mail on the counter, picked up the out going mail and turned to leave. Thinking about my next delivery I reached behind me with my right hand for the door knob.

My heart froze.

What I had hold of did not feel like any door knob I had ever felt. Still, not even daring to breath I looked over my right shoulder at exactly what I was holding. At the same time the lady standing at that rack was also looking over her right shoulder at what I was holding.

What I was holding was that ladies bottom. If I looked as silly as I felt it must have been awful silly because I was turning red and my fool mind decided at that moment to take a short vacation and let my face get redder.

Knowing full well that I had to do something and do it fast I let go of what I was holding, I grabbed the damn door knob and still looking eye ball to eye ball with that lady explained the whole thing in one word. "Whoop's"..!

LIMA BEANS AND HAM HOCKS

1 pound bag lima beans

2 ham hocks

Small onion chopped

2 cloves garlic minced

As much water as needed

Being raised in a small town you soon know all the good places to eat. In our small town we had a winner that stood alone when it came to Lima Beans. Some time he served them with corn bread and some time sour dough. You never knew but the beans were always good. Ask him how he make them and he would tell you about a fish he once caught. As far as any one knows he took his recipe with him.

I tried for several years to make beans half as good as his. One day I thought about how the ham flavor was in the bean its self. Aha! Of course. That had to be the answer.

I placed my 2 ham hocks in a pan with water and simmered them for about an hour then set it aside and let the liquid cool. I rinsed my beans and poured that liquid over them and let them soak over night

The next day I cut all of the lean meat off of the hocks and chopped it pretty fine and put it and the other ingredients in the beans. I added some water and cooked the beans slowly.

By golly, that was as close as I was ever going to come so here it is. Enjoy.............................

MEAT BALLS

½ pound hamburger

½ pound sausage

1 small onion chopped

2 cloves garlic minced

¼ cup dried parsley

½ cup parmesan cheese

½ cup bread crumbs

1 egg

Salt and pepper ?

Mix all the ingredients thoroughly. I like to use my hand to get a better mix with the meat. Add a little water if it seems too dry. Makes about 24 meat balls. I use a teaspoon and it lets me size them. I used to fry them in a skillet but I got smart. Now I place them on a cookie sheet and bake them in a pre heated oven at 350 degrees for about 25 minutes. Sometimes I increase everything but the egg and put the extra in a freezer bag for later use.

MOM'S TUNA CASSAROLE

Ingredients

1 12 o/z can tuna

1 15 o/z can whole or cream style corn

1 15 o/z can mushroom soup

3 hands full of regular potato chips

Drain the tuna as dry as possible and put in mixing bowl. Add the can of corn. [whole kernel corn will make your casserole firmer] Add the can of soup and stir until ingredients are blended. Press the ingredients into a glass baking dish. Put the chips in a plastic bag and crush them as fine as you desire. Sprinkle this over your casserole evenly. Bake at 350 degrees for about 20 minutes or until the chips start to turn brown.

NOTE: You can use any size dish. I prefer a deeper one so there is plenty of room for the chips

The thing I liked best about this dish was that she put the potato chips on top.

PEE-WEE

Walking mail men are fair game for animals, kids and any one with a mad on for the Post Office. In this one part of my mail route there was one small business and five small boys.

Summer was wearing itself out and one day the group of boys approached me asking for some rubber bands. That very morning at the Post Office we had a stand up talk. Seems like somewhere in the world a mail man had give some boys some rubber bands and one of them had gotten hurt with one. The word out was do not give out rubber bands. This is what I told these boys and they acted like they understood and were on there way.

I did not see them for a week or so, and one day while walking along a small water balloon landed close to me. Not close enough to get me wet but close enough to get my attention. Looking around I saw nothing to indicate that it had been deliberately thrown at me. Nothing more happened that day. The next day was different. At about the same spot another water balloon landed. This time it was not the surprise I had yesterday so I looked around. Another and another landed nearer to me. Seemed like all the trees and bushes had grown arms and each arm had a hand and each hand had a water balloon. At the post office we had other stand up talks, like try not starting trouble but, if it comes to you handle it with discretion. Well I just started firing rubber bands at all those bush and tree arms. My aim wasn't much better than theirs, and this went on several times over the next two weeks.

Evidently They had had there fun because they became invisible. It was about that time that the post office decided to try me with a jeep, to make me a park and loop route. Having this jeep caused me to restructure my route and those boys were the last thing on my mind.

One day I parked in front of that small business, locked the jeep up and went inside to deliver the mail. After teasing Mary the receptionist and seeing that she had no out going mail I turned and left the building. Two steps out that door I froze in my tracks. All around me were five heavily armed and very dangerous kids. All standing there with there guns drawn, aimed and the hammers eared back. Before me was the Isle of Death. The whole story unfolded before my eyes. The kids had asked for the rubber bands and been refused so they got them anyway. I could only guess at how many rubber bands they had. The one thing that I did know was that I had none..........................

With fear clutching my heart I turned and ran. Not away, but back in the building yelling for Mary to give me some rubber bands. Mary thought I had gone crazy until I asked her to come see what was waiting for me out that door. What she saw was five little "Billy The Kids" just standing there like statues with there guns drawn, aimed and the hammers eared back. Mary was having a harder time trying not to laugh out loud than she was finding me some ammunition. What can be funny about some one about to meet there doom. Me, I just stood there and watched those statues....

Mary finally came up with all the rubber bands she could find and dropped them into my extended hand. That made me feel better until I looked at what she had put in my hand. These things were some thing you take off your morning paper. What those kids had was some magnum power stuff. What I had was like going bear hunting with a BB gun.

Outside they were getting restless and had about decided that I was going to chicken out. They had started calling me names, especially this real ugly one they called Pee Wee. He was getting nasty saying things like scared cat afraid cat and so on. Name calling doesn't go far with me.

Once again looking at that locked jeep just setting there waiting for me, I knew it would be pure suicide making a run for it. What I had here was a fight that could not be ignored. Checking over my meager supply of ammunition I did find one pretty good one. What I had to do is take out that loud mouth with my first and best shot. Maybe that would take some of the fire out of the rest of them and my chances would be much improved.

Mustering up all the courage I had in me I charged out that door. Sure enough I nailed old loud mouth with that first shot but he was the only one that didn't score a direct hit on me. I was going to loose and it was going to happen fast and the darndest thing happened.

The real ring leader ran up to me with an arm load of water balloons shouting "come on Dub, lets teach them a lesson." Well all of a sudden I had me some cannon power and was more than ready to use it. The remaining four took off like a herd of dirty turtles and we were right behind them giving them what for.

With all that laughing and screaming the people in the neighborhood just had to have a look. For all I knew they might have been in on the whole thing.

None of us really won or lost that small war but we did learn some things about one another. Today all those kids are fine young men. Fact is that Pee Wee stands over six feet tall and is considered handsome. Wonder who named him Pee Wee ....?

OKIE BURRITO

1 large flour tortilla

Frijoles rojo [red beans]

Chopped onion, red or yellow

Diced tomato

Fried potatoes

Salsa or hot sauce if wanted

Salt and pepper

I played around with this recipe for some time and with a little help from the people eating them this is how it turned out.

I start by spooning beans down the middle of the tortilla and taking a fork and mashing them down flat. Then some potatoes because they take up the most room. Then you can pile on what ever else you desire. Usually one makes a meal for me.

Word has trickled down to me that my daughters have changed the name and my grand children call them

" MOM'S BURRITOS "

PECAN OR WALNUT PIE

These two and that Tamale Pie were mothers favorites

We all waited and salivated for one of these pies. In fact I personally kept her freezer handsomely stocked with pecans and walnuts to ensure all of us would be rewarded.

One time a friend convinced her that she should use bacon grease in her pie crust. Mother did not make that mistake again

2 eggs

1 cup Karo syrup [white]

1/8 tsp salt

1 tsp vanilla

1 cup sugar

2 tbs butter or oleo melted

1 cup nut meats in pieces

Beat eggs, add all other ingredients except the nuts and beat well. Fold in the nuts. Pour into an unbaked pie crust and bake at 350 degrees for 1 hour.

BANANA NUT CAKE

One day when we were kids my best bud and I stopped by the house for a minute. There was nobody home and there was this just made cake. We ate half of it and left. When I got home Mom ask if I knew what had happened to her cake. I answered that Wayne said that it was the best cake he had ever eaten.

Cream together 1 ½ cups sugar, 3 egg yolks and ½ cup shortening. Add 1 ¼ cup ripe banana mashed. Combine and add 3 tbs butter milk and 1 tsp baking soda. Shift together and add 2 cups flour,1 tsp baking powder and a dash of salt. Add 1 cup walnuts chopped and 1 tsp vanilla. Fold in 3 stiffly beaten egg whites. Bake in two 8 or 9 inch pans for about thirty minutes at 350 degrees.

Mother would frost it with powdered sugar icing made with butter

PORK CHOP AND RICE

This is another recipe that my wife Helen introduced to the family a very long time ago and it was an immediate hit.

2 CUPS WATER

1 CUP RICE [ANY KIND]

2 FRIED PORK CHOPS

1 PACKAGE LIPTON INSTANT ONION SOUP

1 10 ¾ OZ CAN MUSHROOM SOUP

Helen cooked the rice and added both soups. She poured it in a baking dish and placed the pork chops on top. She then baked it in a 325 degree oven for about 40 minutes. I made some changes.

Cook the onion soup and add the rice and cook it. Chop up the meat on the chops and along with the other can of soup add them to the rice. Put this in a 2 quart baking dish and bake for 35 minutes in a pre heated 325 degree oven.

PIGS IN THE BLANKET

Mother always made these with too much biscuit dough. There would be a small hole at each end or no hole at all. You could not see the wiener and I complained to no avail. I had to wait until I had my own kitchen before any changes would ever take place.

I roll out my dough as square as I can and cut it in one inch strips that I wrap loosely around the wiener and you can see a lot of meat. Some times I slit the wieners and add cheese. There are a number of things you can do to make them more attractive and tasty.

You will have to do it a few times to get it the way you like. When they are prepared place them on a slightly oiled cookie sheet and bake at 450 degrees for about 10-12 minutes.

My Two Dad's

Let me begin with how I have so many Moms and Dads. Mother and Daddy AKA Mom and Dad stuck it out for 25 years. Mother was a very domineering person and Dad just got all of it he could stand and threw in the towel. They did part friendly. It did not take too long until they each had found some one to fill the void. Dad found a women who owned 5 acres out in the country and she promised him that she would put his name on the title if he would only marry her. Dad took hook, line and sinker. What she wanted was a dummy to work the place and 5 acres is just enough land to kill you if you try making a living off it.

Mom for the first time ever started going to some of the better bars in town. I don't know if she was looking for a husband or just lonely. Any way she found her self a man. None of the 4 involved knew that Dad and Bert were friends of sorts so they all just accepted it for what it was and got married to each other. In many ways Dad and Bert were a lot a like

Dad was a tall fat man and Bert was a short fat man and they both like to wear stripped overalls and gnaw on meat bones. Together they could build a house from the ground up but neither one had ever done any of it for a living. Common sense was what they were full of. Dad had a third grade education and I believe if he had gone at least to the ninth grade he would have been the smartest one in the family.

The story about them and me doing some thing together is about to begin. I was a mail man who owned a 100 year old house that I was reverberating, so work was what I knew best. I had taken a two week vacation to paint that old house. This story starts on Saturday at the end of the first week.

"This is all unfair" is what my wife Helen was standing there saying to me while I was cleaning my paint brush. What is I asked? You, all you do is work. You take vacations from work to do more work and there is never any time left for you. Your father is retired and has time on his hands. Your mother is in Texas because of your grand mothers health so Bert is just sitting in Bakersfield twiddling his thumbs. After supper to night I want you to call each of them and tell them you are going fishing Monday morning and it will not be any where local. You will be gone for upwards to a week or less and you want them to accompany you.

Boy-O-Boy did they ever jump at that. In fact they were ready to leave right now. Helen took her cue and visited her favorite market and came home with a whole chicken and a bag of chicken backs and necks. She asked me to cut up the whole chicken and she started frying chicken. We were going to be well fed.

Bert drove up Sunday evening. He and Dad both had campers and I had the boat. We chose Bert's camper because it was the larger of the two and set about preparing for our fishing trip. 6 AM would be here before we knew it. Helen ?, She was still frying chicken...........................!

Boat in tow the three of us were headed north on route 99 to a lake none of us had ever fished in let alone seen. The 99 split's the great San Joaquin Valley from north to south. There are mountains on both sides. The ones to the east are tall and called the Sierra Nevada range. They go from Mexico to Canada. The ones to the west are the coast range and run along the Pacific Ocean. California is a beautiful state with lots to look at and I was just sitting there wondering how the people who built this long and much traveled high way could have missed it all when one of the dads started complaining about being hungry. Bert stopped when he found a road side camp ground. We ate some fried chicken and potato salad Helen had prepared for us. We washed it down with cool water. We can make coffee after we get to where we are going. We have some serious fishing on our minds. We washed up and were on our way.

Lake McClure is big and spread out a lot. It was late when we made camp. The boat could wait until morning. We fished from the bank while we had more fried chicken and salad. This time we had some hot coffee to help it all down.

The coffee did not keep the two dads from getting sleepy and with the luck we were not having you would have to believe the fish were sleepy too. So we just put all our gear away and went to bed and went to sleep.

All three of us were early risers so it was no surprise when we all started getting up just before day light. Don't want to waist any day light sleeping. Bert said he needed to relieve him self and Dad said some thing about washing his face so I volunteered to make some coffee. When I had the coffee going I happened to look down at the lake and low and behold there were my two dads fishing. I hope Bert did not relieve him self in the lake before Dad could wash his face. Yeah right. Dub they just elected you to be there chief cook and bottle washer. Helen is right. All I do is work. Well I intended to put a stop to this business with out saying a word. What little air movement there was, was going there way so I knew they could smell the morning coffee brewing so I put some bacon in the skillet and added some more aromas for them to savor.

"Lets Eat"

They dropped there poles and could only imagine bacon, eggs and toast for breakfast as they trudged up to camp. You would have to have seen it to believe the looks of horror they experienced when Dad said he hardly ever ate cold pork and beans for breakfast while Bert announced that he never ate sliced tomatoes for his breakfast. When they could compose them selves they went ahead and ate what they don't usually eat for breakfast knowing they had made one big mistake. That was the day I lost any kitchen privileges I might have had and started enjoying there cooking.

None of us were having any luck at this fishing hole so we had some more fried chicken for lunch and headed out for Tulloch Lake. It wasn't all that far and easy to find. There was a store at the top of the loading ramp and we needed a couple of things. Some supplies and information. I've noticed that every time we have to buy some thing we all come up with a wad of money. Maybe we should open a small bank. Was there a camp spot and the answer was yes. Go strait down the road heading south and it is the last one on the left. Pretty easy huh?

We off loaded the boat and we all took off in different directions. It was a long boat ride but I finally found our camp spot and it was empty. There was a mooring place so I tied up and walked up to camp and sat on a fallen tree and waited and waited. After a half hour or so I got the boat going and went back to the loading ramp. No was the answer when I asked the people at the bottom of the ramp. No one had seen either of them so I trudged up the ramp to the store and asked the lady that ran it. Another no, but she did get on the two way radio and ask around. They were all saying no when guess who walked in. Where the hell have you two been I almost shouted.

"We got lost"

How in blazes can you get lost going strait down a road? I was not going to ask. I was drinking a cold beer when they showed up and to show me that as far as they were concerned the matter was closed they wanted to know if they were to have one too. WOW!

That night we were having more fried chicken when Bert asked me how many backs did this chicken have? Before I could answer Dad declared that it had a neck three feet long. I then knew that we had eaten all the fried chicken we were going to so after supper was finished I thru out what was left and cleaned Helens big Tupper Ware bowl...........

In the boat I was the pilot, Bert was the co-pilot and Dad was the anchor man. These were there choices, not mine. That after noon we were fishing in a spot that looked promising but really wasn't so we decided to move. Anchor up? Yep. Throttle forward I felt a short tug and when I finally looked back I could see my anchor rope flapping along behind us. I could not get away from this place fast enough.

It was already late in the day when we launched the boat so while my two dads started supper I tied up my boat and asked an attendant there if he could recommend a good cat fish hole. He said sure. Just go all the way across the lake and find an inlet. Go up the inlet until we passed under a bridge, drop our anchor and the cat fish would practically jump in the boat. When I reached camp some thing sure smelled good. I wonder if these guys wife's know just how talented they are in a kitchen? While we ate I told them what I had learned and they were ready. At last we were going to catch some fish and have a big fish fry. After all, what else could possibly go wrong.............................?

When we reached the boat Dad sat where I used to store the anchor. I was really tired and told them so. I asked Bert to be pilot and I laid down on the middle bench as best as I could and was soon fast asleep.

When I awoke it was with a start for I knew we had gone aground and it was as dark as the inside of a cow. I could hear voices in the distance so I knew we were some where we did not belong. I asked "what happened"?

Berts answer was that there was still some light when I made a left turn.

LEFT TURN! I was afraid to ask why he made a turn at all when the instructions were to go until we passed under a bridge. What I knew was we needed to get out of where ever we were and try and make camp.

I did not have any running lights. What I did have was a flash light in my tackle box and I hoped the batteries were strong. I stepped out of the boat and turned us 180 degrees hoping to hit some running water. It didn't take long until I could experience going against moving water. We soon reached the inlet we should have been on and I stopped to get organized. The two dads were both talking at once and what I made out was that the inlet was crammed full of rocks and boulders all sizes. Let me think. I'll take the bow with the flash light. Bert will be pilot and Dad he could set in the middle quietly. Bert and I needed to communicate.

With the flash light I took a better look at what we had facing us. I could only gasp at what I saw. How did I ever sleep through this maze. It must have been a lot easier in day light. We must have bounced off every thing there was to bounce off. This was a trip you only wanted to make but once. After what seemed to last a million years we came around a short bend and there was the lake and a long, long way away was a lone night light marking the dock area. We did not speed up excessively for fear there might be another like us with out running lights. Star light and a flash light are not a whole lot of light

When we finally returned to our camp site I happened to over hear the two dads talking and they agreed that there buddy Dub had had about all of them he could handle in one life time. Dad told Bert that they would break camp early in the morning and stop some where and buy me a big breakfast. And that is what we did, after all didn't I have a house that still needed painting.

The End?

POTATO PATTIES

Got some left over mashed potatoes you don't know what to do with. Problem solved. I stirred into the potatoes an egg, some fried onion and some corn meal. I let this set until I could mold it into patties. I fried them in a hot skillet and they were delicious.

You ask how much of any thing? Depends on how much potatoes you have. One egg is usually enough.

Helen's High Chair

"Hurry up and get your clothes changed" is what Helen was saying when I got home from work." Where is the fire I asked?" "We have to get a high chair" was her answer. "We don't have any babies" I answered. "We are going to have a grand baby and you know that once they start there's no telling when or where it will stop". Women have this special way of knowing things that men don't so we just don't argue with them. I got changed out of my post office uniform and asked where we are in such a hurry to get to. Sears, Ward's or? No, no, no. I don't want plastic junk. We are going to the used furniture stores where we will find what I want.

So away we went…………………………………..................

The first two stores were completely void of what we were looking for but the third one was Trader John's. Trader John has experts working for him that are the first ones at the announced yard sales and they get all the good stuff before the general public gets there.

The minute we entered I felt Helen stiffen. Being a pro she never once looked directly at the high chair. Instead she went on a round about route pretending to look at other house hold items but never loosing sight of the intended item.

When we were a few feet away I stepped aside. Helen did not need my help.

The first thing she noticed was that who ever had dusted this morning had not done a very good job and that might mean that the chair had been taking up space for far too long. Stores like to keep their products moving and this one definitely needed to be moved. Helen reached for the price tag, looked at it and dropped it like it was hot or some thing and said "Ha."

Now that she had stopped the sales person made his move." This won't take long he probably was thinking. That thing wasn't doing any thing other than collecting dust and now was a good time to get rid of it."

When his mouth fell open I knew that Helen had made her opening bid. He stepped back a half step repeating the word no several times. This is not the way that fast sales are supposed to go so he needed to stall a few seconds and regroup.

This is where Helen starts to make her move. She crosses her arms over her chest and being a couple inches over normal for a women and he being a few inches shorter than the average man made it look like she was looking down her nose at him. When he dropped his price it must have been awful small because her eye brows shot strait up. This sale was going south and he knew it.

With one finger on her right hand she reached over and wiped it in the remaining dust. She took a long look at it and then she showed it to him and made her final offer. Not even waiting for an answer Helen opened her purse and started taking out the money she had offered. "Dub, come put this in your truck," is what she said to me and we went home.

SALMON PATTIES

1 7.5 O/Z CAN SALMON

1 TBS DRIED ONION

1 LARGE EGG SLIGHTLY BEATEN

CRACKER CRUMBS

Do not drain, just dump the can contents in a bowl and break it up. Add the rest of the ingredients and mix thoroughly. Let it set for a half hour or so and it will thicken. I usually make four patties and brown them in hot grease.

I like creamed corn on mine with some salad and a slice of bread.........

SHRIMP COCKTAIL

½ PINT SALSA

8 O/Z CAN TOMATO SAUCE

1 TSP WORCESTERSHIRE SAUCE

¼ TSP CELERY SALT

1 TSP CHILI POWDER

1 POUND SHRIMP

In a sauce pan put in all the ingredients but the shrimp and heat to an almost boil. Put the shrimp in the containers you intend serving and fill them ¾ full. Pour the hot sauce and fill to almost full. Set aside and allow to cool. Place in the refrigerator until ready to serve.

Bean's

My wife Helen and I were watching television one evening when our three growing up daughters entered and addressed us. They looked serious and a little bit afraid. When I asked if there was a problem they answered that there certainly was. "We eat too many bean's." It is embarrassing when we are in public. The oldest one was old enough to have a social life. The middle one had a semi social life and the youngest was still wishing for one.

I asked them if we could have a few minutes alone while keeping as straight faced as possible. We needed to discuss this problem. After they left the room we realized that it was a serious problem. We could not tell them that bean's were a big item on our budget. Rice would have to take there place until our finance problem improved.

We called them back in and told them the plan. We would have bean's on Saturday. Most of there out side activities were on Saturday and they usually included food. They all agreed to give the plan a try.

Year's later, when they had there own kids to provide for, each one of them has gone into the kitchen straight to the frig and asked, " Don't you guys ever eat beans?" Of course we do. On Saturday night.

SOUPS

CHICKEN AND NOODLE

After the roasted chicken or turkey is gone you will be amazed at how much meat is still on the bones. I pull them apart and put them in a large pot, cover them with water, put the lid on and simmer this for an hour or so. When this has cooled down I start removing the meat from the bones. Throw the bones away. Use your grease separator and get rid of the grease. Put the meat back in the pot and add some diced onion, garlic, celery and carrots. Put the lid on and make sure you get these done. Then you add 2-3 oz noodles and cook them. Salt and pepper to taste.

CHICKEN AND DUMPLINGS

If you want to make dumplings instead of using noodles just follow the directions on the Bisquick box exactly and you will be in for a real treat.

VEGETABLE AND BEEF SOUP

There was a time you could ask your butcher for a Knuckle and he would give you one. This is what you need to make a really good pot of soup. Then we went through a period of time that it seemed like cattle had no bones. Ask your butcher for a bone and he would tell you that this is the way he gets it, no bones

Now they do have soup bones so get one and cut all the meat off it and put the meat and bone in the pot and cook slowly for 30 or 40 minutes. Remove the bone and pour in I can of mixed vegetables and 1 can of petit canned tomatoes. I always add some chopped onion and garlic or any veggie that I happen to have. Use your imagination and there are a lot of things you can change to make it your soup

Remember those meat balls we put in the freezer? Instead of a bone, cook the meat balls, put them in the soup and call it "Meat Ball Soup".....................!

YELLOW TOMATOES

It was the spring of 1943 and I had just earned my first dollar that I had to pay into Social Security. I had 97 cents when I entered this store that sold about every thing. What had my interest was in the seed rack. Small bell shaped yellow tomatoes. I had to have some of these. I forked over a dime and headed home.

We had an old wash tub that had a hole in the bottom and should have been hauled off to the dump long ago. We also had a milk cow I some times wished some one would haul her off. Being the boy in the family had its goods and bad sides. Any way I mixed some cow droppings and dirt into that old tub and planted my seed. Wow, you needed to stand back. Now I know how Jack felt when he planted his magic beans. You never saw any thing grow the way those tomatoes did. I think every one of those seed took root. They were blooming in no time and I believe that every bloom set.

Boy-o-boy were they ever good. In no time at all we were eating them twice a day and enjoying them. WW2 was raging on and summer was about to wear its self out and we were getting sick to any kind of tomato. I was afraid mother was going to start serving them for breakfast so I started coming to breakfast rather cautious.

One morning I went out to tend to my tomato patch and it was gone. Not just the tomatoes but the tub and all. It was like they had never been there at all. I guess some one with authority must have gotten all the yellow bell shaped tomatoes they wanted. I was so happy they were gone I never asked about there disappearance. What, with all those smiling face's.

SPAGHETTI SAUCE

1 14.5 o/z can petit cut tomatoes

1 can water

1 6 o/z can tomato paste

½ cup diced onion

2 cloves garlic minced

2 tsp olive oil

1 tbs basil leaves

½ tbs chili powder

Put the olive oil in your spaghetti sause pot and sautee the onion and garlic. Add the tomatoes and water. Bring to a gentle boil. Add the tomato paste and stir until mixed well. Simmer a while then add the other ingredients and simmer some more. Add your cooked meat balls and serve.

I have a special way to get tomato paste and cranberry sauce out of the can. Cut the top of the can off and turn the can up side down over what ever you are going to put it in and using the opener make a hole in the bottom like you were going to cut it off too. Blow into that small hole and it usually will just shoot out. Now that you have had a good laugh try it.

CORKY THE GUIDE DOG

Every one that goes to work at the Post Office starts out as the bottom substitute whether they are a carrier or a clerk. As a carrier-sub I soon found out that I had a few favorite routes that I enjoyed the most. This is a story about one of them.

This route was a walking route. The hardest thing about a walking route is finding the mail boxes or mail slots. This was my first time on this route, so I had my work cut out for me. About forty five minutes into the route out came the most amazing dog. She was large, friendly and turned out to be a "guide dog." I tried desperately to shoo her away, but she would have none of that. I finally gave up and decided that she was going to spend the day with me regardless to what I wanted.

Watching her I realized what she was leading me to every mail delivery whether they got mail or not. This was an old zig-zag type route where you crossed back and forth across the street. Boy, not having to search and know when to zig or zag was making this easy. Corky had this route down pat and I would too in short order.

About two hours into the route there was a little old lady who during fare weather hung her parrot cage in a tree in the front yard. Suddenly Corky made a right turn down a side street; I hurried to see why. Hanging in that tree was the cage with the parrot inside. Corky leaped at the cage and gave a friendly bark. The parrot squawked and the little old lady, with a twinkle in her eyes, ran out and scolded Corky. It seemed like she sure got out there in a hurry like maybe she was waiting inside the door. Like maybe this was something she looked forward to each day.

About noon we came upon this drive-in. Corky immediately lay down beside the door as though she belonged there. Regular customers at the restaurant spoke in a friendly manner and Corky wagged her tail. Well I thought, this must be where the regular eats his lunch. I almost wore my neck out watching to see that that dog didn't run off. I still needed her help for the last half of that route.

At the end of the route Corky turned with a smile and a wag of her tail headed home. I went back to the Post Office looking forward to carrying this route again Corky's owners tried several times when she was younger to break her of going with the mail man, but Corky was determined so they gave in to her. She lived a long and healthy life. One day the regular came in saying "Corky did not show up today."

This story about Corky the guide dog is now a part of life the past has claimed and all of us that knew her will surely miss her.

A Nickel

It was a hot day and Helen and I were out and about running errands. Helen decided we should have something cold to drink so I pulled into the first drive through I came to and ordered two small soda's.

When I pay for some thing it makes me happy if I can pay exactly. This time I was a nickel short. The passenger door in our car had an ash tray and Helen used it to hold all the change I picked up in parking lots.

I asked to borrow a nickel.

A week later we were going to town. I stopped at the club house to get the mail. There lying on the side walk was a shiny new dime. I picked it up and when I got in the car I gave it to Helen saying to her that I was paying her back the nickel I had borrowed.

I stopped at the red light at Moony Boulevard and Helen asked "let me get this strait. You borrowed a nickel and paid back a dime?"

Yep...................................

When I stopped at the light at Caldwell avenue she reached over and patted me on my right leg and at the same time she told me that, "The next time you need to borrow a nickel, you come see me first."

STUFFED HAMBURGER

I have just been toying with this for a short while but it is so good that I want to share it with you.

Start with 8 six inch squares wax paper. Make 4 two inch balls of hamburger and place them on squares of paper. Cover them with remaining paper. I use an iron skillet to mash them to about 5 inch diameter. Spread your stuffing to about ½ inc from the edge. Put the remaining meats on top and once again using your skillet flatten them to 5 inches. They cook well in an oven on a cookie sheet. 325 degrees for about 30 minutes.

Meat Pie

1 green onion minced fine

I small clove garlic minced fine

2 tbs grated cheese

1/8 tsp dry mustard.

Stir this up well. Some time I add a little horseradish . I'll bet with a little imagination you can come up with your own stuffing.

1 pound lean hamburger

1 8 o/z can tomato sauce

1 15 o/z can Veg All

1 can water

This is so easy. Crumble the hamburger in a skillet and fry it till it is done. Scrape the meat away from the edge and tilt the skillet until the excess grease collect then wad up a paper towel to sponge the grease out and throw in in the trash. Pour the sauce and water in and stir it well. Add the Veg All and stir again. Let this cook slowly for a little while and let the liquid cook down a little. Pour this into a baking dish that will hold it and top with biscuits. Either homemade or store bought. Place in a heated 425 degree oven for about 15 minutes. I use a large spoon to serve them. You will have to do it a few times to get the liquid level just right....

The Indian Short's

At this time in my career as a mail man I had a walking route. This was during the summer months. My wife and I had three children and never enough money so I was moon lighting at a convenience store to help make ends meet.

One evening one of my mail patrons came into the store to tell me that she and a good friend were going to Washington State to visit some of her family. Starting Monday I was just to shove the mail through the mail door mail slot and hold anything that would not fit at the Post Office.

She was a church friend and a school teacher who was nearing retirement who lived in a very old house by the library.

Monday morning I dressed and went to work. I cased the mail and was out delivering the mail when I became aware that I had on a pair of Indian shorts. You know, the kind that keep sneaking up on you all day. You cannot imagine how silly a person looks walking down the street pulling at there inseam for just a little relief from those ever creeping shorts.

About half way through my route I realized that I was almost to Bessie's house. When I got there I knew exactly what I was going to do. The old house she lived in was built about five feet off the ground. All around the porch was some kind of ivy that completely enclosed the front porch. No one could see me there....................

It had been some time since I had sneaked a pull on my inseam for some much needed comfort so you can imagine the kind of pain I was in. I climbed those stairs two at a time seeking the privacy I so dearly needed.

I shoved the mail through the mail slot, dropped my mail bag off my left shoulder and dropped my pants.

The door opened!!!

The door "SHUT."

By now those darn shorts had climbed so high they were cutting off my air supply. I did not have time to worry about Bessie. I grabbed two hand full of those shorts and after a brief struggle managed to get them down far enough to gulp down some much needed air into my starving lungs. Another good yank and they gave up and were down where they belonged.

With my pants up and satisfied that I could finish my route before I lost all the circulation in my legs for ever I knocked on the door. During all the commotion going on I had not heard Bessie walk away.

Bessie opened the door and I asked her what she was doing at home? It seemed like her friend was sick and she had opened the door to tell me that they were not going until the next Monday. Knowing that she was curious as to why when she opened the door her mail man was standing there with his pants around his ankles I explained it to her. She had a good laugh.

Two years later Bessie retired, sold her house to the city and moved up to Washington State . I told her good-bye, and wanting to avoid this topic of conversation, wished her well and turned to leave. Bessie stopped me long enough to tell me about all the good laughs she gets when she tells about the time she opened the door and there stood her mail man, well you know the rest..............!

TACOS

I definitely do not make tacos like my Dad did. He put some of his suet laden chili on a corn tortilla, fold it over and put tooth pick in to hold it and into the hot grease it went. Oh! Oh! They were so good when you put all the good stuff in, They just were not to good for you. Once in a while was O.K.

It depends on how many are going to be eating at my table. I like to use a big cutting board, chop the tomato, onion and lettuce. Make sure I have plenty of shredded cheese and I am in business. My chili is pretty much suet less so were ready to go. All we need now is salsa.

When I was delivering the mail and we had tacos the night before I put all the left over veggies and cheese in a container and took it for my lunch the next day. It is just too darn hot here in the San Joaquin Valley during the summer to eat a heavy sandwich.

This is another of my Dad's recipes with as much grease removed as possible. His generation were evidently grease eaters. YUK!!!!!!!!!!!

1 dozen corn or flour tortillas

3 cloves garlic minced

1 medium yellow onion chopped

2 cups grated cheese

2 cups chili

1 15 o/z can of enchilada sauce

I use a 7 inch by 11 inch baking dish. Heat the chili. This will help remove grease too. You can usually find tortillas in your grocery store that are so fresh they are soft and will roll up with out breaking. Mix your garlic into the onion. You decide how much of each you want in with chili and roll it up. After the bottom layer is finished, pour some of the sauce on it and put some of your cheese there too. Do the top layer and use all the sauce you have. Place in a pre heated oven [350] and bake for 35 minutes. Good eating.

Meeting Helen

Meeting Helen for the first time was a experience you only have once and then you never forget it. Helen was walking toward the car I was sitting in. I thought that here comes the mother to my children. I looked away. When I looked back at her I realized that I was already in love with her and always had been. I just needed to come face to face with her to know this to be true. Why had it taken me so long to find her?

The reason I was where I was, was because I was on a blind date. We had all four been roller skating and had worked up an appetite. One of the girl's in the car commented that Helen had one of the new "poodle cut" hair cuts.

" Can I run my fingers through your poodle?" That was what I was asking her when she reached the car.

"You will have to ask your wife" is what she answered.

"I don't have a wife" was my answer to that.

Her head tilted forward and every one in the car caught there breath and watched as my hand reached out the window and actually touched that beautiful hair.

Life returned to normal when the deafening silence was broken with her voice asking how she could help us.

How does a person experiencing love for the first time sleep when they can't seem to close there eye's and relax and stop thinking about there new found love. How do they eat? How can they even think about food for crying out loud. It is already past my bed time and 6AM comes around every morning with out fail and Uncle Sam expects me to be out of bed and on the job at seven and here I am wide awake and can't even close my eyes with out seeing her out side that window.

The next thing knew I was waking up and worrying about whether I had just dreamed this beautiful person into my life or was she real and I was going to be able to see her again.

My best buddy Cooper was not with me last night so I could not ask or even tell him about what happened until I see her again and know she is really real. We had some thing to eat and I had a whole day of wondering and waiting ahead of me and no one to talk to about what was going on. She just had to be real.

I had just returned to the State's after spending twenty one month's and nine days in a place called Okinawa where good ole American girl's were very scarce and I was still reeling over the "Dear John" letter I had received unexpectedly one day. There are two things that can happen to a man that he never really gets over. One is a DJ letter and the other is a kick in the ball's. Both hurt equally bad and are hard to forget.

The day lasted for about a million years. Lunch time came and went with out me. By then I was pretty wound up and food was not some thing I could handle right then. Every time I thought about what might happen tonight a big gray cat stood up in my stomach and turned around before it laid back down. I was learning what nervous was all about.

Coop tried to get me to go and eat some supper but I assured him that I would eat later. Before I could discuss any of this with him I had to know the whole truth. Was she real or just some thing I dreamed? Can this be that special person I have unknowingly been waiting for?

Well I am going to find the answer to that in about an hour. Shower, shampoo, shave and shine and then?

Woah up boy. Remember where you are and what you are. You are an air-man stationed at Walker Air Base in Roswell New Mexico and along with local police they also have military police so lets not start out with a speeding ticket. If she is real she will be there when you get there.

Pulling into the drive-in I saw two other pretty girls working but not the girl of my dreams. This hurts. While I was sitting there feeling let down and dumb a noise got my attention. It was her and she was standing at the passenger door looking even more beautiful than before asking me to unlock the door.

With speed any athlete hopes for and it even amazed me how that door flew open and she just seemed to float into my car saying some thing about this being her night off and her name was Helen.

I wanted to do a dozen things all at once like hold her, kiss her, touch her.............

Instead I just sat there like I was frozen in the seat and I was only able to look at her. We were both seeing the same thing at the same time. Two people falling in love for the first time. We both had that same look and we were both looking.

My car was a 1949 Mercury and Helen was the first girl to sit in it. The car had stick shift and over drive that aided in long trips by saving gas and drag racing. Get that bad boy in second gear over drive and the race was yours. Loosing a race never occurred to me. Winning did.

I thought Helen fit into my car like a missing piece to a jig saw puzzle. Especially when that puzzle piece scooted over next to me and said, "Let's go some where." That was not going to be easy. When her left thigh touched my right leg I thought I was going to die. I was like a transmission locked in gear. I don't know when I stopped breathing but my lungs were starting to burn so I let a little air in. Some thing went through me like a bolt out of heaven. Some thing I had never experienced before. Wow this was going to take some getting used too and I had the rest of my life but I did not want to waste any thing.

Helen had been living in Texas with some friends until her mother passed away and she came home. I too had just arrived and running smack dab into this beautiful part Indian Girl who looked every part the Indian she was and proud of it.

Helen must of sensed that I was having trouble breathing because she moved over far enough that we weren't touching any longer and I gulped down some air and began breathing regularly. She asked if I knew where the Bottomless Lakes were. At that moment in time I did not even know where main street was so I just shook my head no.

"When you are ready just turn left here on second street and go about five miles to the top of Comanche Hill" was all she said.

My ears stopped ringing and my stomach muscles loosened enough that I could turn and look at what was really going on.

Helen just sat there with that Mona Lisa smile I was going to grow fond of and waited me out. She probably was wondering what I was eventually going to say.

I was going to learn that Helen was not a talker but when she did speak it paid to be listening. This was going to be the case for the next forty nine and one half years. Unbeknown to either of us they were not going to be easy years. Trying years would better describe them.

Quit mussing Dub and say some thing intelligent. Just sitting here looking like you just fell off a turnip wagon is not getting the job done.

" The Bottomless Lakes huh. Lets see if I can find them."

And all our years together began. By the time we reached those infamous lakes we were talking like good friends and over the years that is what we became.

THANKSGIVING

[DRESSING]

My favorite time of the year is when I can show off my corn bread dressing. I started cooking this a very long time ago and the complaints are few. One thing I believe that makes it so good is that it is made from old bread. What you do is save that last piece of corn bread or those few biscuits by sticking them in a large freezer bag and they will add up.

Put all the jiblets in a pan with 2 cups water. In another pan put 1 cup diced onion 1 cup diced celery and 2 cups water. Cook these slowly so that you will not loose much of the liquid. You also need 2 large boiled eggs. While these are cooking and the turkey is in the oven take a large bowl and crumble the bread. How much bread you use is determined by how many people. The more you make this the better it will get.

When the giblets are done cut all of the meat off of the neck and dice with the rest of the meat. Mix them and divide in half. Half for the dressing and the rest for the giblet gravy. Pour in half the giblet water and all the onion/celery and stir it all up. This will not be enough liquid but there is more on the way when that turkey is ready.

There are two spices other than salt and pepper that you will use. Poultry seasoning and Sage. Some people can't handle too much sage and some none at all so ask around before you get too frisky. Chop your eggs and I personally like and use a can of drained green olives. If someone doesn't like them they can set them aside.

When the turkey is done remove it from the pan and get your grease separator if you have one. Pour the liquid from the pan into it and separate the grease. Pour at least half of the liquid into it in the gravy pan and use as much of it as you need to make the dressing almost runny. Pour it into the turkey pan and put it in the hot oven and bake until it starts to brown around the edges

The Watermelon Patch

C.Q. Charge of Quarters is one of the perks that come along with being a sergeant. It is my first time and I am pretty nervous about it. In the orderly room alone waiting for the telephone to ring and some one tells you that WW111 has just begun. My job then is tell the first sergeant. That's it. This will turn out to be the longest and strangest night of my life.

5 PM

It is time for my night-mare to begin and it won't end until 7 AM. I picked up some food at the P X, not a lot but enough too keep me from starving. Later on if I filled up I would surely fall asleep and that is a big no no. A Court Martial offense no no

The first few hours were easy because I had remembered to bring the book I was reading. Sitting in the 1st Sergeant's chair reading was neat. I got up every once in a while and walked inside or out side. I don't remember darkness falling but it had and I think this was the first time since I had arrived on Okinawa that I was completely alone. This place is 35 miles long and 3 miles wide at it's widest place and right now seemed completely void of another human being.

I made a pot of coffee and while it was perking I peered out side and saw nothing but a few night lights away over there. Boy, that coffee tastes good. I ate a little of my food supply

12AM

Wow, it's the middle of the night and reading is not working now. It has the opposite effect and is making me sleepier. Seven more hours and I am wondering what I should do to help me make it. I made some more coffee and ate a small amount of food.

I walked out side and just stood their staring into the night darkness. I have no idea what I expected to see. When I went back inside it was 1 AM and I might as well just lay myself down on the floor and die. I don't think I have ever been this sleepy. My eyes feel gritty like there is sand in them. Hey, I'll bet that if I closed my eyes they wouldn't hurt any more, and I would be sound asleep. Maybe I could figure a way for only one eye to sleep at a time. The problem with that is which eye gets to go first. I'm really getting confused. My life is flashing before me and I am surely going to die. I'm too young too die. God said I could hang around for three score and ten, what ever the heck that is supposed too mean. He never had to pull C Q. Too busy creating I guess. This is all getting dumber by the minute.

The weather here is warm and cool with no fog so rushing out side for a cold blast of night air is out of the question.

Wonder what is in this desk. Probably pens, pencils and paper and stuff like that.

Slide.....Yep.....Slam!

Slide.....Yep.....Slam!

Slide. WHAT THE ?????????? CONDOMS ??????????

There must be a thousand condoms in this drawer. What can I do with a thousand rubbers. Haven't heard a word about them so there will be a stand up talk advising us to carry a little protection when going to town.

" SNAP "

The building I am in is an old metal Quonset hut and they are always making some sort of noises. I looked not knowing what to expect in the direction the noise had come from and saw three used C O 2 fire extinguishers that needed refilled. When they are full there is a seal telling you they are ready for use. I have used one and I know that if you hold the nozzle steady and pull the trigger you will get a small pile of snow and that is what I did.

I am awake now !

I opened one of the condoms and put some snow in it. To this I added water, tied a knot on the open end and tossed it on the floor and waited. I did not have to wait long. The darn thing inflated it's self and looked like a small foot-ball.

I emptied all three of the fire extinguishers and had a good pile of snow. Grabbed a container full of water, located a teaspoon and went to work.

7 AM

Ready or not a new day was beginning and I had not died of lack of sleep. Coffee was perking and I was reared back in sergeant Gallagher chair watching 50 or so condom filling with air and looking like a water melon patch when in he walks. Or rather he stops. He could not believe what he was seeing. Then he espied me relaxing in his chair and croaked out for me to get the HELL out of here.

While I was at the mess hall having a small breakfast I mulled over what had happened last night and figured out that all the first sergeants get together over a pitcher of beer and laugh like a bunch of mean little boys about the thing the guy on C Q has to do just to stay awake.

The End

TUNA SALAD

I WAS INFORMED BY ONE OF MY CHILDREN THAT I WAS THE ONLY PERSON SHE KNEW OF THAT PUTS BOILED EGGS IN THEIR TUNA SALAD. I ALSO ADD SOME CELERY AND I ADD THESE MOSTLY BECAUSE IT HELPS MAKE THE SALAD TO FEED MORE PEOPLE.

1 6 o/z can tuna

1 boiled egg chopped

¼ cup celery chopped fine.

Enough mayonnaise so it will hold together

PEA SALAD

I guess it was only natural for a kid to roll his peas around on his plate hoping they would magically dissapear.

I was one of those and it usually took a hard stare or two to get my attention. I then would mash them all together and eat them as swiftly as possible.

One day Mother solved that problem forever by introducing Pea Salad. I hoped it was her idea but she never said. What she did was chop some lettuce, add a can of drained peas and some mayo. How much of each depends on how big you want your salad. I personally added some chopped onion and they go well. Now I eat peas any way I can.

A SUMMER SALAD

THIS IS A SURPRISINGLY VERY GOOD SALAD. ALL HE DID WAS DICE SOME TOMATO, ONION AND CUCUMBER AND MIX SOME OIL, VINEGAR AND WATER TO POUR ON WITH A DASH OF SALT AND PEPPER

MUSTARD POTATO SALAD

The secret to making a really good potato salad is making sure that all the potatoes are all the same size . When you use a tooth pick to see if one is done and it is , then they are all done. I never buy deli salad. I dice my potatoes, chop some onion, chop a boiled egg, add some dill relish and then half mayo and half mustard. I grew up on salad made with sweet relish and lots of mayonnaise.

MEMORIES

Can you believe that I have been here for 101 years and my sun burst out front shines even when it is raining. Lovely I am not. Lived in I am. That's right, I am a house. The things I have seen and heard while just standing here would fill volumes. Some good and some bad. You would not believe the memories I hold inside.

Just last night my now owner was out front in the yard working when an elderly lady and an almost grown grand son were walking by when suddenly granny looked up and pointed at me and said "that is a ghost house and the one over there is to." I looked over there to see if that other house had heard. Taking a long look I wandered if any of my ghosts had ever gone over there and if they did, why? The big dumb looking kid said "ah heck there aint no ghosts." Well granny answered right back that she ought to know because her and some friends had played in them one time when they were both setting empty. Granny was right for now that I study on it she was the one that always slammed the doors trying to scare the ghosts out of me. Little did she know that my soul was born when the first nail was pounded into me and my ghosts are here to stay'

When I first landed in the neighborhood and it was almost country, there were not many like me around. You know, Colonial. Wow, was I impressive setting here on an acre of land. There were trees and shrubs galore and a big lawn to mow. I was called the "W.F. Thomas Farm House."

Things were great for a long time and I just stood here and took it all in. Like when "WW1" came along and things got a little shaky all over the world. It was to be the war to end all wars. We endured it and in fact we won it and it ended on 11/11/1918. That became a national holiday. We still celebrate it but it is now called Veterans Day because we have so many veterans. The economy picked up and things were really humming along until 1929. That is when Wall Street fell and the Great Depression started.

Things got worse in a hurry. We did not know what we were in for. Hard times were a coming.

This is about the time that I and a lot of other big and old houses became the infamous ghost houses. It could not be helped. There was a big expense for the up keep on a big old house and money was definitely in short supply. Why the Thomas family left me I am not sure but they left me setting empty and lonely. There were some tenants from time to time but none of them were paying rent and they did not stay long. They were people with no where else to be and land lords knew that houses lived in lasted longer than empty ones did. Not liking it was one thing, putting up with it was some thing else.

Things were a lot worse than I thought. It seemed like a long time before any real changes took place. In fact it took "WW2" to put a stop to the awful Depression. We won that war too. The only thing was we had to fight dirty and use an Atomic Bomb to get Japan's attention.

Not only being out of the depression, I had a new owner. Mr. and Mrs. Neil. A middle aged couple and boy were they nice to me. Right off the bat I received a paint job and did it feel good. During the time I stood here lonely and steadfast some realtors were busy reducing my yard space. All of a sudden new and different type houses were popping up all over the place.

Mr. Neil was a black smith or Ferrier or some thing like that. There is still a carriage house across the street. Probably the only one left in town. One day when no one was looking Mr. Neil passed away. Mrs. Neil had a lot of old furniture and some fine memories. Slowly she drew a line around both of us. That only made us both lonely. Finally she could not take the lonely any more. She made a duplex of sorts out of the house and a nice lady named Mrs. Upchurch moved in the apartment. They had a good relationship for a lot of years. Time has a way stealing your youth and your gusto. Suddenly there were two elderly ladies living here and keeping up with the maintenance was proving to be to difficult.

A very long time ago when some one wall papered, first they had to hang cheese cloth on the walls. This was because of some impunities in the walls like cracks and so on. Then they applied the glued paper. By now the wall paper was out weighing the cheese cloth and the fact that they had papered the ceiling that stuff was hanging every where. Some industrious person had tried tacking it back up and that made it worse. The paint inside and out side was in desperate need of repair. A couple of my many windows were either cracked or broken so it was in evident that Mrs. Neil had run out of energy and could no longer live here with me. Knowing what was in store for me my only prayer was that she did not leave me empty again. I was so used to having people around that the mere mention of them not being there was enough to make me cry. I could all most see those mean little kids running through me slamming doors.

For a number of years I had had my eye on the mail man. He would show up at about the same time every work day and you could just see that look on his face. He liked that old house. He had always been friendly with both ladies of the house and they were friendly right back. Then what I knew was going to happen happened. Mrs. Neil put me up for sale.

What I did not know was that Mrs. Upchurch had run into the mail man on his appointed rounds and told him the house was for sale. It just so happened that the realtor handling the sale was also on his route. When he arrived there he asked Mr. Olson if he would hold off advertising the pending sale. He told the mail man he had two weeks. This means that I will not have to suffer the indignity of having an ugly for sale sigh stuck in my front yard. Mr. Olson went about his business and never let on to me that he had a prospect.

Mr. Mail man bought his wife and an older couple over and they all four looked me over something awful. They even saw things I was trying to hide. This may sound silly, but some thing made of solid red wood and is as old as I am has some modesty. If they would have looked carefully under the pealing paint, they would have seen me blush. What caused me to not throw a fit and fall down on them was the fact that they went away happy.

After a few days of pure hell, like me not knowing any thing, I could almost feel the need for a stiff drink. You see no one had ever told Mrs. Neil or any one else that I could see and feel. Having the sneaky feeling that a new owner was in my near future, I just settled down on my red wood frame and waited.

I knew that the mail man had it in him and sure enough he decided that he could handle the task of restoring me. You see, this is the first time I had any thing to do with picking a owner.

We went through a week or so of relatives coming over and saying I want this and I want that. Finally Mrs. Neil stood up as tall as gravity would allow her to stand and told the whole bunch that she was going to give the rest of the stuff to her mail man.

Boy did that ever make me happy. You would not believe what items they had hauled off. You never see those type people until some one dies and they can get some thing for nothing. They went away grumbling so good riddance. Heck, I had lived with that furniture for years and had become accustomed to having it around.

I did not stay empty or idle for long. The mail man and his wife showed up and did a lot of talking and measuring. They were making some sort of plans and it was hard for me to hear, so I had to suppose.

Two days later they showed up again, only this time they had three teen age daughters with them. I do not remember this as being part of the deal. Maybe I should have set Mr. Mail man down and inquired about his family.

Ouch! I can still remember that old gal out front bragging about how she used to play inside of me. What kind of misery am I in store for? Liking the mail man and his wife and not knowing any thing about the teenagers, I decided to wait and see.

Standing there pouting and pretending that I did not know what was going on inside me, I got this warm feeling. Not wanting them to know that I cared I just kept doing what I was good at. Pouting.

Oh! What they as a family were doing to me had a marvelous feeling. Suddenly that tacky wall paper that was sagging all over the pace was removed and replaced with some new wall paper. By now wall paper had been improved so much that there was hardly nothing to it. No more cheese cloth and thick paste. Just wet it and put it on. Try as I might I could not see every thing they were doing, but it sure felt good. I could feel myself starting to relax.

Hot dog! Here was a big truck in front and a lot of people and I knew that they were moving in. What they had done to me so far was just enough so they could move in. Now we will see what my future looks like.

You could not believe all the banging of hammers, sawing, painting and all the things that were going on inside and out side of me. Me, I was keeping an eye on those girls. Not really knowing them gave me cause to worry.

The new owner had been at it for about five years when his middle daughter started acting ugly. The mail man and his wife were stymied. Finally they sent her to the family doctor. I have always been able to get along with doctors but this one was about to test my strength. What he did was to tell Mom and Dad that this girl needed her own room and her own door to slam. I think I have already make my self clear about how I feel about door slamming.

The mailman asked his Dad who was a handy mans handy man to help him. He was retired at the time and was just messing around on five acres north of town. I had a back porch and the mail man wanted his dad to look at it and see if it could be made into a bed room. This guy could build a house from the ground up but had never practiced being a carpenter for a living. Looking closely he estimated that they could do the job for about two hundred dollars.

Dad said he had a couple of windows for the north wall and two leaded glass doors for the east end. Said it would help make the morning sun prettier and Patti would like waking up to that. Me I am old and here they are talking modern down there. What will the other old houses in the neighborhood have to say about this? I need to think.

Wow! The mail man and his dad got busy in a hurry. He had to use another week of his vacation time but I'm sure it will be worth it. They were almost finished one morning when the intended tenant stepped inside for a look. What she saw was the skeleton of the closet and some bare studs. The paneling had not been picked up yet. With a sniff of air the little brat went to school. Dad and the mail man doubled there efforts. I guess they had had about all of my attitude they could stand. See I wasn't the only one with an attitude. When the grouch came home to her very own bed room for the first time in her life was ready and waiting for her. All that was left was for her and Mrs. Mail man to go down and pick out the carpet and the right color of paint. I wished I had seen her face when she first saw it. She had no idea how hard a lot of people worked to make all this possible.

Have you ever wondered why very pretty girls get up in the morning and spend hours trying to make them selves look different?

I only had two electrical circuits when they moved in. Now that I was a four bed room house and each of the girls occupied there own space I just knew that the mail man was going to go broke buying fuses. You can not believe how many modern contraptions it takes to turn a pretty face into another pretty face.

Those girls plugged a million things into one circuit and "poof" there would go another fuse. Fuss as he would, nothing was going to stop those girls from plugging in every thing that was pluggable.

Destitute and facing bankruptcy for sure he made his move. If you can not bring the mountain to Mohamed, then you take Mohamed to the mountain. Mail man took another week of vacation time and this time he called upon his step father for the much needed help. Like his father this guy could also build a house from the ground up. Bert was a whiz at electrical stuff so he came willingly ready to help. A good friend of mine was a licensed electrician so with Bert and I doing the work and my friend checking it all out we rewired the house.

Crawling around under me the mail man found an abandoned cellar. Back in the fifties there was a big flood and it had filled with water so no one ever went back down there. In fact some one had laid linoleum over the trap door.

With all kinds of electricity all over the house in every room things started to get back to some kind of normalcy. There was even a separate line for the washing machine.

Suddenly radios started blaring, hair driers started blowing. Curling irons started smelling. I had never experienced the awful odor of burning hair. So many things going on that I wasn't surprised that the doors started slamming again. This is what life is all about with three girls.

Mail man was spending a lot of time out side painting me. If you think that didn't feel good. I had been completely redone inside and now it was time for the out side. Inside I had new kitchen cupboards. The old ones were so awful that mail man used them to make the garage into a work shop. With all the work he was doing and had in store he needed a shop. A lot of wall paper and some paint, with some new furniture that went very well with the old. Not being able to see inside me to well, I have often wondered how I looked and matched. It sure did not take long for me to get to liking those girls. It seemed like I can not remember having children living in me. I just hoped the mail man would not let them be mean to me.

The girls started dating and bringing around some pretty nice guys. One by one they left home. Some to college and some to seek there place. Careers were being found and so were husbands. Some how they had survived there puberty years and there dad. All turning out to be nice young ladies.

You can't believe all the tiny little feet running around inside me laughing and playing and just having a good time. Every once in a while I hear Mrs. Mail man threatening to skin one of them alive, but I don't for one minute believe her. I don't think the ones being threatened do either because they always laugh with glee. I do wish that the grand children could take it easy on me front screen door. One by one they have each managed to push it out and each time mail man takes it down and replaces the screen wire and tells them to knock it off. I have also seen the paper boy take a shot or two at it.

I could go on and tell you stories for ever but it would take up to much time. I have been listening real close lately and am afraid that I am hearing the same old story again. Now that the girls are all gone and are raising there own families it makes it mighty lonely around here. The mail man is about to retire and spending the rest of his life working on me just isn't in his plans. He will have fish to catch and places to go.

I cannot say that I am pleased to think whats in my future, but lets face it. The mail man has been good to me and deserves a break. Maybe there is another young family out there that has the gumption on the monumental task of keeping me up to some kind of standards

Shoot, I wont even complain if they have kids. Fact of the matter is that I have grown found of them ....!

TUNA AND NOODLE SURPRISE

1 12 o/z can tuna drained

4 o/z noodles cooked

1 10 3/4 o/z can mushroom soup

1 tsp oleo or butter

1 tsp all purpose flour

1/4 cup finely diced celery some milk

In a pan melt the oleo and stir in the celery. cook until celery is transparent. Add the flour and a little milk and make it into a white sauce. Add the tuna and soup. Drain and add the noodles. When mixed well, pour into a 2 quart baking dish and place into a pre heated oven at 350 degrees and bake for 35-40 minutes. It will be bubbling.

NOTE: some times I add some minced onion just to change the flavor some.

Ode To A Lost Love

Though the years have passed

Yet here we still stand

Saying those things at last

We thought were oh so grand

Yet in our hearts this thought will always lie

Eat, drink and be merry tomorrow we may die

Yes tomorrow we may die

Some times a day might be a year

Some time it may be only a day

Yet in our hearts this thought still lies

Eat, drink and be merry for tomorrow we may die